John Greenleaf Whittier

Ballads of New England

John Greenleaf Whittier

Ballads of New England

ISBN/EAN: 9783742899859

Manufactured in Europe, USA, Canada, Australia, Japa

Cover: Foto ©Thomas Meinert / pixelio.de

Manufactured and distributed by brebook publishing software
(www.brebook.com)

John Greenleaf Whittier

Ballads of New England

OF

NEW ENGLAND

BY

JOHN GREENLEAF WHITTIER

WITH ILLUSTRATIONS

BOSTON
FIELDS, OSGOOD, & CO.
1870

THE landscape illustrations in this volume, both principal and accessory, have been drawn chiefly from sketches made by MR. HARRY FENN, who visited for the purpose the scenes of the poems. In offering to the public an edition of these well-known Ballads upon the illustration of which the utmost care has been bestowed, the publishers have much pleasure in presenting the following note from the author : —

"I have examined the sheets of the Ballads, and I find that in truthfulness of illustration, and in beauty and delicacy of execution, the pictures are all that could be desired. In the illustrations to COBBLER KEEZAR'S-VISION, THE WRECK OF RIVERMOUTH, MY PLAYMATE, and THE COUNTESS, especially, I recognize the scenery familiar from boyhood, and which I have endeavored to associate in the mind of the reader of my Ballads with the characters and incidents of local traditions."

JOHN G. WHITTIER.

CONTENTS.

LIST OF ILLUSTRATIONS.

[The Engravings by A. V. S. Anthony, under whose supervision the book is prepared.]

COBBLER KEEZAR'S VISION.

AMY WENTWORTH.

[The Vignettes and Ornaments in the introductory pages are drawn by JOHN HARLEY.]

TELLING THE BEES.

H ERE is the place ; right over the hill
    Runs the path I took ;
You can see the gap in the old wall still,
    And the stepping-stones in the shallow brook.

There is the house, with the gate red-barred,
    And the poplars tall ;
And the barn's brown length, and the cattle-yard,
    And the white horns tossing above the wall.

There are the beehives ranged in the sun ;
    And down by the brink
Of the brook are her poor flowers, weed-o'errun,
    Pansy and daffodil, rose and pink.

A year has gone, as the tortoise goes,
  Heavy and slow ;
And the same rose blows, and the same sun glows,
  And the same brook sings of a year ago.

There 's the same sweet clover-smell in the breeze ;
  And the June sun warm
Tangles his wings of fire in the trees,
  Setting, as then, over Fernside farm.

I mind me how with a lover's care
  From my Sunday coat
I brushed off the burrs, and smoothed my hair,
  And cooled at the brookside my brow and throat.

Since we parted, a month had passed,
  To love, a year ;
Down through the beeches I looked at last
  On the little red gate and the well-sweep near.

I can see it all now, — the slantwise rain
  Of light through the leaves,
The sundown's blaze on her window-pane,
  The bloom of her roses under the eaves.

Just the same as a month before, —
  The house and the trees,
The barn's brown gable, the vine by the door, —
  Nothing changed but the hives of bees.

Before them, under the garden wall,
  Forward and back,
Went drearily singing the chore-girl small,
  Draping each hive with a shred of black.

Trembling, I listened: the summer sun
   Had the chill of snow;
For I knew she was telling the bees of one
   Gone on the journey we all must go!

Then I said to myself, " My Mary weeps
   For the dead to-day:
Haply her blind old grandsire sleeps
   The fret and the pain of his age away."

But her dog whined low; on the doorway sill,
   With his cane to his chin,
The old man sat; and the chore-girl still
   Sung to the bees stealing out and in.

And the song she was singing ever since
   In my ear sounds on: —
" Stay at home, pretty bees, fly not hence!
   Mistress Mary is dead and gone!"

MY PLAYMATE.

THE pines were dark on Ramoth hill,
　　Their song was soft and low :
The blossoms in the sweet May wind
　　Were falling like the snow.

The blossoms drifted at our feet,
　　The orchard birds sang clear ;
The sweetest and the saddest day
　　It seemed of all the year.

For, more to me than birds or flowers,
　　My playmate left her home,
And took with her the laughing spring,
　　The music and the bloom.

She kissed the lips of kith and kin,
　　She laid her hand in mine :
What more could ask the bashful boy
　　Who fed her father's kine ?

She left us in the bloom of May :
　　The constant years told o'er
Their seasons with as sweet May morns,
　　But she came back no more.

I walk, with noiseless feet, the round
   Of uneventful years ;
Still o'er and o'er I sow the spring
   And reap the autumn ears.

She lives where all the golden year
   Her summer roses blow ;
The dusky children of the sun
   Before her come and go.

There haply with her jewelled hands
   She smooths her silken gown, —
No more the homespun lap wherein
   I shook the walnuts down

The wild grapes wait us by the brook,
   The brown nuts on the hill,
And still the May-day flowers make sweet
   The woods of Follymill.

The lilies blossom in the pond,
   The bird builds in the tree,
The dark pines sing on Ramoth hill
   The slow song of the sea.

I wonder if she thinks of them,
   And how the old time seems, —
If ever the pines of Ramoth wood
   Are sounding in her dreams.

I see her face, I hear her voice :
   Does she remember mine ?
And what to her is now the boy
   Who fed her father's kine ?

What cares she that the orioles build
   For other eyes than ours, —
That other hands with nuts are filled,
   And other laps with flowers ?

O playmate in the golden time !
 Our mossy seat is green,
Its fringing violets blossom yet,
 The old trees o'er it lean.

The winds so sweet with birch and fern
 A sweeter memory blow ;
And there in spring the veeries sing
 The song of long ago.

And still the pines of Ramoth wood
 Are moaning like the sea, —
The moaning of the sea of change
 Between myself and thee !

SKIPPER IRESON'S RIDE.

O F all the rides since the birth of time,
    Told in story or sung in rhyme, —
On Apuleius's Golden Ass,
Or one-eyed Calendar's horse of brass,
Witch astride of a human hack,
Islam's prophet on Al-Borák, —
The strangest ride that ever was sped
Was Ireson's, out from Marblehead!
    Old Floyd Ireson, for his hard heart,
    Tarred and feathered and carried in a cart
    By the women of Marblehead!

Body of turkey, head of owl,
Wings a-droop like a rained-on fowl,
Feathered and ruffled in every part,
Skipper Ireson stood in the cart.

Scores of women, old and young,
Strong of muscle, and glib of tongue,
Pushed and pulled up the rocky lane,
Shouting and singing the shrill refrain:
  "Here 's Flud Oirson, fur his horrd horrt.
  Torr'd an' futherr'd an' corr'd in a corrt
    By the women o' Morble'ead!"

Wrinkled scolds with hands on hips,
Girls in bloom of cheek and lips,

Wild-eyed, free-limbed, such as chase
Bacchus round some antique vase,
Brief of skirt, with ankles bare,
Loose of kerchief and loose of hair,
With conch-shells blowing and fish-horns' twang,
Over and over the Mænads sang :
   " Here 's Flud Oirson, fur his horrd horrt,
    Torr'd an' futherr'd an' corr'd in a corrt
      By the women o' Morble'ead ! "

Small pity for him ! — He sailed away
From a leaking ship, in Chaleur Bay, —
Sailed away from a sinking wreck,
With his own towns-people on her deck !
" Lay by ! lay by !" they called to him.
Back he answered, " Sink or swim !
Brag of your catch of fish again !"
And off he sailed through the fog and rain !
   Old Floyd Ireson, for his hard heart,
    Tarred and feathered and carried in a cart
      By the women of Marblehead !

Fathoms deep in dark Chaleur
That wreck shall lie forevermore.
Mother and sister, wife and maid,
Looked from the rocks of Marblehead

Skipper Ireson's Ride.

Over the moaning and rainy sea, —
Looked for the coming that might not be!
What did the winds and the sea-birds say
Of the cruel captain who sailed away? —
   Old Floyd Ireson, for his hard heart,
    Tarred and feathered and carried in a cart
      By the women of Marblehead!

Through the street, on either side,
Up flew windows, doors swung wide;
Sharp-tongued spinsters, old wives gray,
Treble lent the fish-horn's bray.
Sea-worn grandsires, cripple-bound,
Hulks of old sailors run aground,
Shook head, and fist, and hat, and cane,
And cracked with curses the hoarse refrain:

" Here 's Flud Oirson, fur his horrd horrt,
Torr'd an' futherr'd an' corr'd in a corrt
     By the women o' Morble'ead ! "

Sweetly along the Salem road
Bloom of orchard and lilac showed.
Little the wicked skipper knew
Of the fields so green and the sky so blue.

Riding there in his sorry trim,
Like an Indian idol glum and grim,
Scarcely he seemed the sound to hear
Of voices shouting, far and near :
     " Here 's Flud Oirson, fur his horrd horrt,
     Torr'd an' futherr'd an' corr'd in a corrt
        By the women o' Morble'ead ! "

" Hear me, neighbors ! " at last he cried, —
" What to me is this noisy ride ?

What is the shame that clothes the skin
To the nameless horror that lives within?
Waking or sleeping, I see a wreck,
And hear a cry from a reeling deck!
Hate me and curse me, — I only dread
The hand of God and the face of the dead!"
 Said old Floyd Ireson, for his hard heart,
 Tarred and feathered and carried in a cart
  By the women of Marblehead!

Then the wife of the skipper lost at sea
Said, "God has touched him! — why should we?"
Said an old wife mourning her only son,
"Cut the rogue's tether and let him run!"
So with soft relentings and rude excuse,
Half scorn, half pity, they cut him loose,
And gave him a cloak to hide him in,
And left him alone with his shame and sin.
 Poor Floyd Ireson, for his hard heart,
 Tarred and feathered and carried in a cart
  By the women of Marblehead!

COBBLER KEEZAR'S VISION.

THE beaver cut his timber
    With patient teeth that day,
The minks were fish-wards, and the crows
    Surveyors of highway, —

When Keezar sat on the hillside
    Upon his cobbler's form,
With a pan of coals on either hand
    To keep his waxed-ends warm.

And there, in the golden weather,
    He stitched and hammered and sung ;
In the brook he moistened his leather,
    In the pewter mug his tongue.

Well knew the tough old Teuton
　Who brewed the stoutest ale,
And he paid the goodwife's reckoning
　In the coin of song and tale.

The songs they still are singing
　Who dress the hills of vine,
The tales that haunt the Brocken
　And whisper down the Rhine.

5

Woodsy and wild and lonesome,
The swift stream wound away,
Through birches and scarlet maples
Flashing in foam and spray, —

Down on the sharp-horned ledges
Plunging in steep cascade,
Tossing its white-maned waters
Against the hemlock's shade.

Woodsy and wild and lonesome,
East and west and north and south;
Only the village of fishers
Down at the river's mouth;

Only here and there a clearing,
  With its farm-house rude and new,
And tree-stumps, swart as Indians,
  Where the scanty harvest grew.

No shout of home-bound reapers,
  No vintage-song he heard,
And on the green no dancing feet
  The merry violin stirred.

"Why should folk be glum," said Keezar,
  "When Nature herself is glad,
And the painted woods are laughing
  At the faces so sour and sad?"

Small heed had the careless cobbler
  What sorrow of heart was theirs
Who travailed in pain with the births of God,
  And planted a state with prayers, —

Hunting of witches and warlocks,
  Smiting the heathen horde, —
One hand on the mason's trowel,
  And one on the soldier's sword!

But give him his ale and cider,
  Give him his pipe and song,
Little he cared for Church or State,
  Or the balance of right and wrong.

-

"'T is work, work, work," he muttered, —
  "And for rest a snuffle of psalms!"
He smote on his leathern apron
  With his brown and waxen palms.

"O for the purple harvests
  Of the days when I was young!
For the merry grape-stained maidens,
  And the pleasant songs they sung!

" O for the breath of vineyards,
  Of apples and nuts and wine !
For an oar to row and a breeze to blow
  Down the grand old river Rhine ! "

A tear in his blue eye glistened,
  And dropped on his beard so gray.
" Old, old am I," said Keezar,
  " And the Rhine flows far away ! "

But a cunning man was the cobbler ;
  He could call the birds from the trees,
Charm the black snake out of the ledges,
  And bring back the swarming bees.

All the virtues of herbs and metals,
 All the lore of the woods, he knew,
And the arts of the Old World mingled
 With the marvels of the New.

Well he knew the tricks of magic,
 And the lapstone on his knee
Had the gift of the Mormon's goggles
 Or the stone of Doctor Dee.

For the mighty master Agrippa
 Wrought it with spell and rhyme
From a fragment of mystic moonstone
 In the tower of Nettesheim.

To a cobbler Minnesinger
 The marvellous stone gave he, —
And he gave it, in turn, to Keezar,
 Who brought it over the sea.

He held up that mystic lapstone,
 He held it up like a lens,
And he counted the long years coming
 By twenties and by tens.

" One hundred years," quoth Keezar,
  " And fifty have I told :
Now open the new before me,
  And shut me out the old ! "

Like a cloud of mist, the blackness
  Rolled from the magic stone,
And a marvellous picture mingled
  The unknown and the known.

Still ran the stream to the river,
  And river and ocean joined ;
And there were the bluffs and the blue sea-line,
  And cold north hills behind.

But the mighty forest was broken
  By many a steepled town,
By many a white-walled farm-house,
  And many a garner brown.

Turning a score of mill-wheels,
  The stream no more ran free ;
White sails on the winding river,
  White sails on the far-off sea.

Below in the noisy village
  The flags were floating gay,
And shone on a thousand faces
  The light of a holiday.

Swiftly the rival ploughmen
  Turned the brown earth from their shares ;
Here were the farmer's treasures,
  There were the craftsman's wares.

Golden the goodwife's butter,
 Ruby her currant-wine ;
Grand were the strutting turkeys,
 Fat were the beeves and swine.

Yellow and red were the apples,
 And the ripe pears russet-brown,
And the peaches had stolen blushes
 From the girls who shook them down.

And with blooms of hill and wild-wood,
 That shame the toil of art,
Mingled the gorgeous blossoms
 Of the garden's tropic heart.

"What is it I see?" said Keezar,
 "Am I here, or am I there?
Is it a fête at Bingen?
 Do I look on Frankfort fair?

" But where are the clowns and puppets,
    And imps with horns and tail ?
And where are the Rhenish flagons ?
    And where is the foaming ale ?

" Strange things, I know, will happen, —
    Strange things the Lord permits ;
But that droughty folk should be jolly
    Puzzles my poor old wits.

" Here are smiling manly faces,
    And the maiden's step is gay ;
Nor sad by thinking, nor mad by drinking,
    Nor mopes, nor fools, are they.

" Here 's pleasure without regretting,
    And good without abuse,
The holiday and the bridal
    Of beauty and of use.

" Here 's a priest and there is a Quaker, —
    Do the cat and dog agree ?
Have they burned the stocks for oven-wood ?
    Have they cut down the gallows-tree ?

" Would the old folk know their children ?
  Would they own the graceless town,
With never a ranter to worry
  And never a witch to drown ? "

Loud laughed the cobbler Keezar,
  Laughed like a school-boy gay ;
Tossing his arms above him,
  The lapstone rolled away.

It rolled down the rugged hillside,
  It spun like a wheel bewitched,
It plunged through the leaning willows,
  And into the river pitched.

There, in the deep, dark water,
　The magic stone lies still,
Under the leaning willows
　In the shadow of the hill.

But oft the idle fisher
　Sits on the shadowy bank,
And his dreams make marvellous pictures
　Where the wizard's lapstone sank.

And still, in the summer twilights,
　When the river seems to run
Out from the inner glory,
　Warm with the melted sun,

The weary mill-girl lingers
 Beside the charméd stream,
And the sky and the golden water
 Shape and color her dream.

Fair wave the sunset gardens,
 The rosy signals fly ;
Her homestead beckons from the cloud,
 And love goes sailing by !

AMY WENTWORTH.

H ER fingers shame the ivory keys
    They dance so light along ;
The bloom upon her parted lips
    Is sweeter than the song.

O perfumed suitor, spare thy smiles !
    Her thoughts are not of thee ;
She better loves the salted wind,
    The voices of the sea.

Her heart is like an outbound ship
    That at its anchor swings ;
The murmur of the stranded shell
    Is in the song she sings.

She sings, and, smiling, hears her praise,
　But dreams the while of one
Who watches from his sea-blown deck
　The icebergs in the sun.

She questions all the winds that blow,
　And every fog-wreath dim,
And bids the sea-birds flying north
　Bear messages to him.

She speeds them with the thanks of men
　He perilled life to save,
And grateful prayers like holy oil
　To smooth for him the wave.

Brown Viking of the fishing-smack !
    Fair toast of all the town ! —
The skipper's jerkin ill beseems
    The lady's silken gown !

But ne'er shall Amy Wentworth wear
    For him the blush of shame
Who dares to set his manly gifts
    Against her ancient name.

The stream is brightest at its spring,
    And blood is not like wine ;
Nor honored less than he who heirs
    Is he who founds a line.

Full lightly shall the prize be won,
    If love be Fortune's spur ;
And never maiden stoops to him
    Who lifts himself to her.

Her home is brave in Jaffrey Street,
    With stately stairways worn
By feet of old Colonial knights
    And ladies gentle-born.

Still green about its ample porch
   The English ivy twines,
Trained back to show in English oak
   The herald's carven signs.

And on her, from the wainscot old,
   Ancestral faces frown, —
And this has worn the soldier's sword,
   And that the judge's gown.

But, strong of will and proud as they,
   She walks the gallery floor
As if she trod her sailor's deck
   By stormy Labrador !

7

The sweetbrier blooms on Kittery-side,
And green are Elliot's bowers;
Her garden is the pebbled beach,
The mosses are her flowers.

She looks across the harbor-bar
To see the white gulls fly;
His greeting from the Northern sea
Is in their clanging cry.

She hums a song, and dreams that he,
  As in its romance old,
Shall homeward ride with silken sails
  And masts of beaten gold !

O, rank is good, and gold is fair,
  And high and low mate ill ;
But love has never known a law
  Beyond its own sweet will.

THE COUNTESS.

OVER the wooded northern ridge,
    Between its houses brown,
To the dark tunnel of the bridge
    The street comes straggling down.

You catch a glimpse, though birch and pine,
    Of gable, roof, and porch,
The tavern with its swinging sign,
    The sharp horn of the church.

The river's steel-blue crescent curves
    To meet, in ebb and flow,
The single broken wharf that serves
    For sloop and gundelow.

With salt sea-scents along its shores
　The heavy hay-boats crawl,
The long antennæ of their oars
　In lazy rise and fall.

Along the gray abutment's wall
　The idle shad-net dries :
The toll-man in his cobbler's stall
　Sits smoking with closed eyes.

You hear the pier's low undertone
　Of waves that chafe and gnaw ;
You start, — a skipper's horn is blown
　To raise the creaking draw.

At times a blacksmith's anvil sounds
　With slow and sluggard beat,
Or stage-coach on its dusty rounds
　Wakes up the staring street.

A place for idle eyes and ears,
    A cobwebbed nook of dreams,
Left by the stream whose waves are years
    The stranded village seems.

And there, like other moss and rust,
    The native dweller clings,
And keeps, in uninquiring trust,
    The old, dull round of things.

The fisher drops his patient lines,
    The farmer sows his grain,
Content to hear the murmuring pines
    Instead of railroad train.

Go where, along the tangled steep
    That slopes against the west,
The hamlet's buried idlers sleep
    In still profounder rest.

Throw back the locust's flowery plume,
    The birch's pale-green scarf,
And break the web of brier and bloom
    From name and epitaph.

A simple muster-roll of death,
    Of pomp and romance shorn,
The dry, old names that common breath
    Has cheapened and outworn.

Yet pause by one low mound, and part
    The wild vines o'er it laced,
And read the words by rustic art
    Upon its headstone traced.

Haply yon white-haired villager
    Of fourscore years can say
What means the noble name of her
    Who sleeps with common clay.

An exile from the Gascon land
  Found refuge here and rest,
And loved of all the village band
  Its fairest and its best.

He knelt with her on Sabbath morns,
  He worshipped through her eyes,
And on the pride that doubts and scorns
  Smile in her faith's surprise.

Her simple daily life he saw
  By homeliest duties tried,
In all things by an untaught law
  Of duteous justified,

For her his rank aside he laid;
  He took the hoe and tone
Of lowly life and toil, and made
  Her simple ways his own.

Yet still in gay and careless ease,
  To harvest-field or dance
He brought the gentle courtesies,
  The nameless grace of France.

Ah ! life is brief, though love be long ;
  The altar and the bier,
The burial hymn and bridal song,
  Were both in one short year !

Her rest is quiet on the hill,
  Beneath the locust's bloom :
Far off her lover sleeps as still
  Within his scutcheoned tomb.

The Gascon lord, the village maid,
  In death still clasp their hands ;
The love that levels rank and grade
  Unites their severed lands.

What matter whose the hillside grave,
  Or whose the blazoned stone ?
Forever to her western wave
  Shall whisper blue Garonne !

O Love ! — so hallowing every soil
  That gives thy sweet flower room,
Wherever, nursed by ease or toil,
  The human heart takes bloom ! —

Plant of lost Eden, from the sod
   Of sinful earth unriven,
White blossom of the trees of God
   Dropped down to us from heaven ! —

This tangled waste of mound and stone
   Is holy for thy sake ;
A sweetness which is all thy own
   Breathes out from fern and brake.

And while ancestral pride shall twine
   The Gascon's tomb with flowers,
Fall sweetly here, O song of mine,
   With summer's bloom and showers !

And let the lines that severed seem
   Unite again in thee,
As western wave and Gallic stream
   Are mingled in one sea !

MARY GARVIN.

FROM the heart of Waumbek Methna, from the lake that
    never fails,
Falls the Saco in the green lap of Conway's intervales ;
There, in wild and virgin freshness, its waters foam and flow,
As when Darby Field first saw them, two hundred years ago.

But, vexed in all its seaward course with bridges, dams, and
    mills,
How changed is Saco's stream, how lost its freedom of the
    hills,
Since travelled Jocelyn, factor Vines, and stately Champer-
    noon
Heard on its banks the gray wolf's howl, the trumpet of the
    loon !

With smoking axle hot with speed, with steeds of fire and
      steam,
Wide-waked To-day leaves Yesterday behind him like a dream.
Still, from the hurrying train of Life fly backward far and fast
The milestones of the fathers, the landmarks of the past.

But human hearts remain unchanged : the sorrow and the sin,
The loves and hopes and fears of old, are to our own akin ;
And if, in tales our fathers told, the songs our mothers sung,
Tradition wears a snowy beard, Romance is always young.

O sharp-lined man of traffic, on Saco's banks to-day !
O mill-girl watching late and long the shuttle's restless play !
Let, for the once, a listening ear the working hand beguile,
And lend my old Provincial tale, as suits, a tear or smile !

———

The evening gun had sounded from gray Fort Mary's walls ;
Through the forest, like a wild beast, roared and plunged the
      Saco's falls ;

And westward on the sea-wind, that damp and gusty grew,
Over cedars darkening inland the smokes of Spurwink blew.

On the hearth of Farmer Garvin blazed the crackling walnut
      log ;
Right and left sat dame and goodman, and between them lay
      the dog,

Head on paws, and tail slow wagging, and beside him on her
 mat,
Sitting drowsy in the fire-light, winked and purred the mottled
 cat.

"Twenty years!" said Goodman Garvin, speaking sadly, under
 breath,
And his gray head slowly shaking, as one who speaks of
 death.

The goodwife dropped her needles : "It is twenty years
 to-day
Since the Indians fell on Saco, and stole our child away."

Then they sank into the silence, for each knew the other's
 thought,
Of a great and common sorrow, and words were needed not.

" Who knocks ? " cried Goodman Garvin. The door was open
  thrown ;
On two strangers, man and maiden, cloaked and furred, the
  fire-light shone.

One with courteous gesture lifted the bear-skin from his head ;
" Lives here Elkanah Garvin ? " " I am he," the goodman
  said.

" Sit ye down, and dry and warm ye, for the night is chill
  with rain."
And the goodwife drew the settle, and stirred the fire amain.

The maid unclasped her cloak-hood, the fire-light glistened
  fair
In her large, moist eyes, and over soft folds of dark brown
  hair.

Dame Garvin looked upon her : " It is Mary's self I see !
Dear heart ! " she cried, " now tell me, has my child come
  back to me ? "

" My name indeed is Mary," said the stranger, sobbing wild ;
" Will you be to me a mother ? I am Mary Garvin's child !

" She sleeps by wooded Simcoe, but on her dying day
She bade my father take me to her kinsfolk far away.

" And when the priest besought her to do me no such wrong,
She said, 'May God forgive me! I have closed my heart too
    long.

"'When I hid me from my father, and shut out my mother's call,
I sinned against those dear ones, and the Father of us all.

"'Christ's love rebukes no home-love, breaks no tie of kin
    apart ;
Better heresy in doctrine, than heresy of heart.

"'Tell me not the Church must censure: she who wept the
    Cross beside
Never made her own flesh strangers, nor the claims of blood
    denied ;

"'And if she who wronged her parents with her child
    atones to them,
Earthly daughter, Heavenly mother! thou at least wilt not
    condemn !'

"So, upon her death-bed lying, my blessed mother spake ;
As we come to do her bidding, so receive us for her sake."

"God be praised !" said Goodwife Garvin. "He taketh, and
    he gives ;
He woundeth, but he healeth ; in her child our daughter
    lives !"

"Amen !" the old man answered, as he brushed a tear away,
And, kneeling by his hearthstone, said, with reverence, " Let
    us pray."

All its Oriental symbols, and its Hebrew paraphrase,
Warm with earnest life and feeling, rose his prayer of love
    and praise.

But he started at beholding, as he rose from off his knee,

The stranger cross his forehead with the sign of Papistrie.

"What is this?" cried Farmer Garvin. "Is an English Christian's home

A chapel or a mass-house, that you make the sign of Rome?"

Then the young girl knelt beside him, kissed his trembling hand, and cried:

"O, forbear to chide my father; in that faith my mother died!

" On her wooden cross at Simcoe the dews and sunshine fall,
As they fall on Spurwink's graveyard ; and the dear God
    watches all ! "

The old man stroked the fair head that rested on his knee ;
" Your words, dear child," he answered, " are God's rebuke to me.

" Creed and rite perchance may differ, yet our faith and hope
    be one.
Let me be your father's father, let him be to me a son."

When the horn, on Sabbath morning, through the still and
    frosty air,
From Spurwink, Pool, and Black Point, called to sermon and
    to prayer,

To the goodly house of worship, where, in order due and fit,
As by public vote directed, classed and ranked the people sit ;

Mistress first and goodwife after, clerkly squire before the clown,
From the brave coat, lace embroidered, to the gray frock,
    shading down ;

From the pulpit read the preacher, — " Goodman Garvin and
    his wife
Fain would thank the Lord, whose kindness has followed
    them through life,

"For the great and crowning mercy, that their daughter, from the wild,
Where she rests (they hope in God's peace), has sent to them her child ;

"And the prayers of all God's people they ask, that they may prove
Not unworthy, through their weakness, of such special proof of love."

As the preacher prayed, uprising, the aged couple stood,
And the fair Canadian also, in her modest maidenhood.

Thought the elders, grave and doubting, "She is Papist born
    and bred";
Thought the young men, "'T is an angel in Mary Garvin's
    stead!"

THE RANGER.

ROBERT RAWLIN! — Frosts were falling
  When the ranger's horn was calling
Through the woods to Canada.
Gone the winter's sleet and snowing,
Gone the spring-time's bud and blowing,
Gone the summer's harvest mowing,
  And again the fields are gray.
  Yet away, he 's away!
Faint and fainter hope is growing
  In the hearts that mourn his stay.

Where the lion, crouching high on
Abraham's rock with teeth of iron,
  Glares o'er wood and wave away,
Faintly thence, as pines far sighing,

Or as thunder spent and dying,
Come the challenge and replying,
  Come the sounds of flight and fray.
  Well-a-day! Hope and pray!
Some are living, some are lying
  In their red graves far away.

Straggling rangers, worn with dangers,
Homeward faring, weary strangers
  Pass the farm-gate on their way;

Tidings of the dead and living,
Forest march and ambush, giving,
Till the maidens leave their weaving,
    And the lads forget their play.
    "Still away, still away!"
Sighs a sad one, sick with grieving,
    "Why does Robert still delay!"

Nowhere fairer, sweeter, rarer,
Does the golden-locked fruit-bearer
    Through his painted woodlands stray,
Than where hillside oaks and beeches
Overlook the long, blue reaches,
Silver coves and pebbled beaches,
    And green isles of Casco Bay;
    Nowhere day, for delay,
With a tenderer look beseeches,
    "Let me with my charmed earth stay."

On the grain-lands of the mainlands
Stands the serried corn like train-bands,
    Plume and pennon rustling gay;
Out at sea, the islands wooded,
Silver birches, golden-hooded,
Set with maples, crimson-blooded,
    White sea-foam and sand-hills gray,
    Stretch away, far away.

Dim and dreamy, over-brooded
  By the hazy autumn day.

Gayly chattering to the clattering
Of the brown nuts downward pattering,
  Leap the squirrels, red and gray.
On the grass-land, on the fallow,
Drop the apples, red and yellow,
Drop the russet pears and mellow,
  Drop the red leaves all the day.
  And away, swift away,
Sun and cloud, o'er hill and hollow
  Chasing, weave their web of play.

"Martha Mason, Martha Mason,
Prithee tell us of the reason
  Why you mope at home to-day :
Surely smiling is not sinning ;
Leave your quilling, leave your spinning ;
What is all your store of linen,
  If your heart is never gay ?
  Come away, come away !
Never yet did sad beginning
  Make the task of life a play."

Overbending, till she 's blending
With the flaxen skein she 's tending

Pale brown tresses smoothed away
From her face of patient sorrow,

Sits she, seeking but to borrow,
From the trembling hope of morrow,
    Solace for the weary day.
    "Go your way, laugh and play;
Unto Him who heeds the sparrow
    And the lily, let me pray."

"With our rally rings the valley, —
Join us!" cried the blue-eyed Nelly;
    "Join us!" cried the laughing May:
"To the beach we all are going,
And, to save the task of rowing,
West by north the wind is blowing,
    Blowing briskly down the bay!
    Come away, come away!
Time and tide are swiftly flowing,
    Let us take them while we may!

"Never tell us that you'll fail us,
Where the purple beach-plum mellows
    On the bluffs so wild and gray.
Hasten, for the oars are falling;
Hark, our merry mates are calling:
Time it is that we were all in,
    Singing tideward down the bay!"
    "Nay, nay, let me stay;
Sore and sad for Robert Rawlin
    Is my heart," she said, "to-day."

"Vain your calling for Rob Rawlin!
Some red squaw his moose-meat 's broiling,
    Or some French lass, singing gay ;
Just forget as he 's forgetting ;
What avails a life of fretting ?
If some stars must needs be setting,
    Others rise as good as they."
    "Cease, I pray ; go your way ! "
Martha cries, her eyelids wetting ;
    " Foul and false the words you say !"

"Martha Mason, hear to reason !
Prithee, put a kinder face on ! "
    " Cease to vex me," did she say ;
" Better at his side be lying,
With the mournful pine-trees sighing,
And the wild birds o'er us crying,
    Than to doubt like mine a prey ;
    While away, far away,
Turns my heart, forever trying
    Some new hope for each new day.

"When the shadows veil the meadows,
And the sunset's golden ladders
   Sink from twilight's walls of gray,
From the window of my dreaming
I can see his sickle gleaming,
Cheery-voiced, can hear him teaming
   Down the locust-shaded way;
   But away, swift away,
Fades the fond, delusive seeming,
   And I kneel again to pray.

"When the growing dawn is showing,
And the barn-yard cock is crowing,
   And the horned moon pales away,
From a dream of him awaking,
Every sound my heart is making
Seems a footstep of his taking;
   Then I hush the thought, and say,
   'Nay, nay, he's away!'
Ah! my heart, my heart is breaking
   For the dear one far away."

Look up, Martha! worn and swarthy,
Glows a face of manhood worthy :
   "Robert!" "Martha!" all they say.

O'er went wheel and reel together,
Little cared the owner whither ;
Heart of lead is heart of feather,
   Noon of night is noon of day!
   Come away, come away!
When such lovers meet each other,
   Why should prying idlers stay?

The Ranger.

Quench the timber's fallen embers,
Quench the red leaves in December's
   Hoary rime and chilly spray,
But the hearth shall kindle clearer,
Household welcomes sound sincerer,
Heart to loving heart draw nearer,
   When the bridal bells shall say:
   "Hope and pray, trust alway;
Life is sweeter, love is dearer,
   For the trial and delay!"

THE WRECK OF RIVERMOUTH.

RIVERMOUTH ROCKS are fair to see,
  By dawn or sunset shone across,
When the ebb of the sea has left them free,
  To dry their fringes of gold-green moss:
For there the river comes winding down
From salt sea-meadows and uplands brown,
And waves on the outer rocks afoam
Shout to its waters, "Welcome home!"

And fair are the sunny isles in view
  East of the grisly Head of the Boar,
And Agamenticus lifts its blue
  Disk of a cloud the woodlands o'er;

The Wreck of Rivermouth.

And southerly, when the tide is down,
'Twixt white sea-waves and sand-hills brown,
The beach-birds dance and the gray gulls wheel
Over a floor of burnished steel.

Once, in the old Colonial days,
  Two hundred years ago and more,
A boat sailed down through the winding ways
  Of Hampton River to that low shore,
Full of a goodly company
Sailing out on the summer sea,
Veering to catch the land-breeze light,
With the Boar to left and the Rocks to right.

In Hampton meadows, where mowers laid
  Their scythes to the swaths of salted grass,
"Ah, well-a-day! our hay must be made!"
  A young man sighed, who saw them pass.
Loud laughed his fellows to see him stand
Whetting his scythe with a listless hand,
Hearing a voice in a far-off song,
Watching a white hand beckoning long.

"Fie on the witch!" cried a merry girl,
  As they rounded the point where Goody Cole
Sat by her door with her wheel atwirl,
  A bent and blear-eyed poor old soul.
"Oho!" she muttered, "ye 're brave to-day!
But I hear the little waves laugh and say,
'The broth will be cold that waits at home;
For it 's one to go, but another to come!'"

"She 's cursed," said the skipper; "speak her fair:
  I 'm scary always to see her shake
Her wicked head, with its wild gray hair,
  And nose like a hawk, and eyes like a snake."
But merrily still, with laugh and shout,
From Hampton River the boat sailed out,
Till the huts and the flakes on Star seemed nigh,
And they lost the scent of the pines of Rye.

The Wreck of Rivermouth.

They dropped their lines in the lazy tide,
    Drawing up haddock and mottled cod ;
They saw not the Shadow that walked beside,
    They heard not the feet with silence shod.
But thicker and thicker a hot mist grew,
Shot by the lightnings through and through :
And muffled growls, like the growl of a beast,
Ran along the sky from west to east.

Then the skipper looked from the darkening sea
    Up to the dimmed and wading sun ;
But he spake like a brave man cheerily,
    "Yet there is time for our homeward run."
Veering and tacking, they backward wore ;
And just as a breath from the woods ashore
Blew out to whisper of danger past,
The wrath of the storm came down at last !

The skipper hauled at the heavy sail :
"God be our help!" he only cried,
As the roaring gale, like the stroke of a flail,
    Smote the boat on its starboard side.
The Shoalsmen looked, but saw alone
Dark films of rain-cloud slantwise blown,
Wild rocks lit up by the lightning's glare,
The strife and torment of sea and air.

Goody Cole looked out from her door :
    The Isles of Shoals were drowned and gone,
Scarcely she saw the Head of the Boar
    Toss the foam from tusks of stone.
She clasped her hands with a grip of pain,
The tear on her cheek was not of rain :
"They are lost," she muttered, "boat and crew !
Lord, forgive me ! my words were true !"

Suddenly seaward swept the squall ;
    The low sun smote through cloudy rack ;
The Shoals stood clear in the light, and all
    The trend of the coast lay hard and black.
But far and wide as eye could reach,
No life was seen upon wave or beach ;
The boat that went out at morning never
Sailed back again into Hampton River.

.O mower, lean on thy bended snath,
  Look from the meadows green and low:
The wind of the sea is a waft of death,
  The waves are singing a song of woe!
By silent river, by moaning sea,
Long and vain shall thy watching be:
Never again shall the sweet voice call,
Never the white hand rise and fall!

O Rivermouth Rocks, how sad a sight
  Ye saw in the light of breaking day!

Dead faces looking up cold and white
  From sand and sea-weed where they lay.
The mad old witch-wife wailed and wept,
And cursed the tide as it backward crept:
"Crawl back, crawl back, blue water-snake!
Leave your dead for the hearts that break!"

Solemn it was in that old day
  In Hampton town and its log-built church,
Where side by side the coffins lay
  And the mourners stood in aisle and porch.
In the singing-seats young eyes were dim,
The voices faltered that raised the hymn,
And Father Dalton, grave and stern,
Sobbed through his prayer and wept in turn.

But his ancient colleague did not pray,
  Because of his sin at fourscore years:
He stood apart, with the iron-gray
  Of his strong brows knitted to hide his tears.
And a wretched woman, holding her breath
In the awful presence of sin and death,
Cowered and shrank, while her neighbors thronged
To look on the dead her shame had wronged.

Apart with them, like them forbid,
   Old Goody Cole looked drearily round,
As, two by two, with their faces hid,
   The mourners walked to the burying-ground.
She let the staff from her clasped hands fall :
" Lord, forgive us ! we 're sinners all ! "
And the voice of the old man answered her :
" Amen ! " said Father Bachiler.

So, as I sat upon Appledore
   In the calm of a closing summer day,
And the broken lines of Hampton shore
   In purple mist of cloud-land lay,
The Rivermouth Rocks their story told ;
And waves aglow with sunset gold,
Rising and breaking in steady chime,
Beat the rhythm and kept the time.

And the sunset paled, and warmed once more
　With a softer, tenderer after-glow ;
In the east was moon-rise, with boats off shore
　And sails in the distance drifting slow.
The beacon glimmered from Portsmouth bar,
The White Isle kindled its great red star ;
And life and death in my old-time lay
Mingled in peace like the night and day !

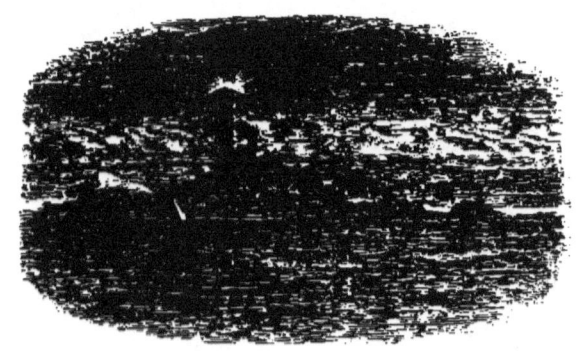

THE CHANGELING.

FOR the fairest maid in Hampton
    They needed not to search,
Who saw young Anna Favor
    Come walking into church, —

Or bringing from the meadows,
    At set of harvest-day,
The frolic of the blackbirds,
    The sweetness of the hay.

Now the weariest of all mothers,
    The saddest two-years' bride,
She scowls in the face of her husband,
    And spurns her child aside.

"Rake out the red coals, goodman,
 For there the child shall lie,
Till the black witch comes to fetch her,
 And both up chimney fly.

"It 's never my own little daughter,
 It 's never my own," she said ;
"The witches have stolen my Anna,
 And left me an imp instead.

"O, fair and sweet was my baby,
 Blue eyes, and hair of gold ;
But this is ugly and wrinkled,
 Cross, and cunning, and old.

" I hate the touch of her fingers,
  I hate the feel of her skin ;
It 's not the milk from my bosom,
  But my blood, that she sucks in.

" My face grows sharp with the torment ;
  Look ! my arms are skin and bone ! —
Rake open the red coals, goodman,
  And the witch shall have her own.

" She 'll come when she hears it crying,
  In the shape of an owl or bat,
And she 'll bring us our darling Anna
  In place of her screeching brat."

Then the goodman, Ezra Dalton,
  Laid his hand upon her head :
" Thy sorrow is great, O woman !
  I sorrow with thee," he said.

" The paths to trouble are many,
  And never but one sure way
Leads out to the light beyond it :
  My poor wife, let us pray."

Then he said to the great All-Father,
　"Thy daughter is weak and blind ;
Let her sight come back, and clothe her
　Once more in her right mind.

"Lead her out of this evil shadow,
　Out of these fancies wild ;
Let the holy love of the mother
　Turn again to her child.

"Make her lips like the lips of Mary
　Kissing her blessed Son ;
Let her hands, like the hands of Jesus,
　Rest on her little one.

"Comfort the soul of thy handmaid,
　Open her prison-door,
And thine shall be all the glory
　And praise forevermore."

Then into the face of its mother
　The baby looked up and smiled ;
And the cloud of her soul was lifted,
　And she knew her little child.

Λ beam of the slant west sunshine
Made the wan face almost fair,
Lit the blue eyes' patient wonder,
And the rings of pale gold hair.

She kissed it on lip and forehead,
She kissed it on cheek and chin,
And she bared her snow-white bosom
To the lips so pale and thin.

O, fair on her bridal morning
  Was the maid who blushed and smiled,
But fairer to Ezra Dalton
  Looked the mother of his child.

With more than a lover's fondness
  He stooped to her worn young face,
And the nursing child and the mother
  He folded in one embrace.

"Blessed be God!" he murmured.
  "Blessed be God!" she said;
"For I see, who once was blinded,—
  I live, who once was dead.

"Now mount and ride, my goodman,
  As thou lovest thy own soul!
Woe's me if my wicked fancies
  Be the death of Goody Cole!"

His horse he saddled and bridled,
  And into the night rode he,—
Now through the great black woodland,
  Now by the white-beached sea.

He rode through the silent clearings,
  He came to the ferry wide,
And thrice he called to the boatman
  Asleep on the other side.

He set his horse to the river,
  He swam to Newbury town,
And he called up Justice Sewall
  In his nightcap and his gown.

And the grave and worshipful justice
  (Upon whose soul be peace !)
Set his name to the jailer's warrant
  For Goody Cole's release.

Then through the night the hoof-beats
  Went sounding like a flail ;
And Goody Cole at cockcrow
  Came forth from Ipswich jail.

www.ingramcontent.com/pod-product-compliance
Lightning Source LLC
Chambersburg PA
CBHW020037030726
47499CB00007B/2465